"The time is now for us to get serious about training Christians to seize everyday opportunities to spread the gospel. This book puts us well on our way to doing just that. I recommend it to anyone who wants to obey Jesus' command to 'go and make disciples.'"

—Daniel L. Akin, president,
Southeastern Baptist Theological Seminary

"I applaud Jimmy and Steve for adapting principles that have started multiplying movements around the world to their South Florida context. I would encourage any Christian who cares about spreading the gospel to read this book, learn from it, and develop a strategy for reaching their city, county, and state."

—Ying Kai, founder of T4T Global Missions,
church planter and pastor, author of
T4T: A Discipleship ReRevolution

"Most Christians understand that Jesus has commanded us to carry the gospel to those who don't yet know Him. But far too many Christians can't imagine how to have those conversations without feeling like a salesman or a cult leader. In this book, Jimmy Scroggins and Steve Wright show the way with practical wisdom. This could light a fire under your personal witness or under the evangelism of your church or ministry."

—Russell D. Moore, PhD, president,
Ethics & Religious Liberty Commission

"I wholeheartedly recommend this book to any pastor or church leader who is interested in seeing the Holy Spirit do a work in their community. I have seen firsthand how the multiplying principles laid out here work. I have also seen firsthand how reproducing and reproducible the 3 Circles is as a gospeling tool. If people put into practice what they read here, I think we will see more and more Americans repent and believe in Jesus. And that fires me up!"

—Jeff Sundell, director of US Strategies,
e3 Partners, Romans 15:23, #NoPlaceLeft

TURNING
EVERYDAY
CONVERSATIONS
INTO
GOSPEL
CONVERSATIONS

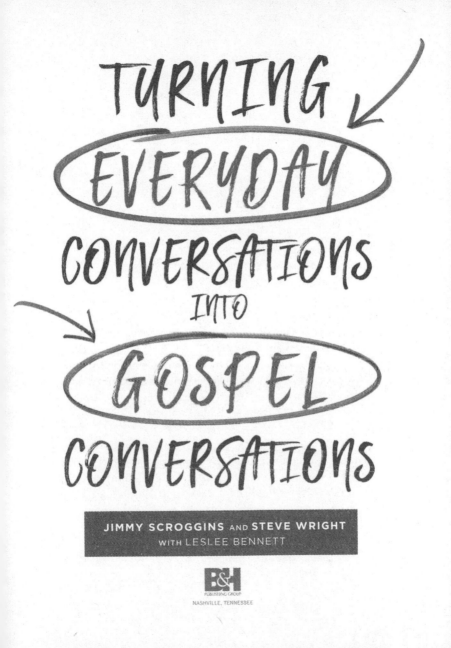

TURNING
EVERYDAY
CONVERSATIONS
INTO
GOSPEL
CONVERSATIONS

JIMMY SCROGGINS AND **STEVE WRIGHT**
WITH LESLEE BENNETT

B&H
PUBLISHING GROUP
NASHVILLE, TENNESSEE

978-1-4627-4784-9

Published by B&H Publishing Group
Nashville, Tennessee

Dewey Decimal Classification: 248.5
Subject Heading: WITNESSING \ GOSPEL \
CHRISTIAN LIFE

7 8 9 10 11 • 22 21 20 19 18

Contents

Acknowledgments

We are thankful that someone took the time to share the gospel with us. Our lives, our families, and our eternity all look different because of gospel conversations. As pastors, we have sought to personally share this amazing good news that has so radically changed our lives. We are grateful to God for the power of the resurrection.

We also want to thank our wives, Kristin and Tina. Both of these women have supported us faithfully, have served daily by our sides, and have been used by God to shape us into the men we have become.

Jimmy Scroggins and Steve Wright
@JimmyScroggins @SteveWright_
#3Circles

An Everyday Gospel for Everyday People

Bill Sullivan wasn't someone you heard preach at a conference. He never wrote a book. He wasn't even a pastor. He was a layperson who believed the gospel had the power to change lives.

One night many years ago, Bill had a gospel conversation with a young, twentysomething couple named Mike and Glenda. They came to faith in Christ that night. A few days later, I stood on a pew and watched my parents get baptized. I never met Bill Sullivan, and at the time I didn't fully understand what my parents did that night, but that gospel conversation changed my parents' lives for eternity.

It changed the trajectory of their three children and thirteen grandchildren too.

I'm forever grateful this ordinary, everyday Christian took the time to have a gospel conversation with my parents all those years ago.

I'm convinced that for the church in North America to make a dent in our continent's lostness, we need more Bill Sullivans. The North American church needs more believers actively engaging their neighbors and coworkers in gospel conversations.

Scripture is clear that the Great Commission isn't just given to a select few trained pastors. It's given to everyone. I'm convinced that more people are interested in hearing the gospel than most Christians are in sharing it.

When I heard what God was doing at Family Church through Jimmy Scroggins and the 3 Circles, I knew this simple way of sharing Christ could dramatically multiply the number of people having gospel conversations throughout North America. To do it, you need no other resources than a pencil and paper. You need no advanced degrees.

The approach you'll read about in this book fits perfectly with what we're trying to do at the North American Mission Board to mobilize Southern Baptists to plant new churches and engage their communities with the gospel. We've already partnered with Jimmy to train Southern Baptists to use the 3 Circles. We've released a smartphone app and print brochure called *3 Circles: Life Conversation Guide.*

We are constantly getting reports on the effectiveness of this tool. We've heard stories of senior citizens and young children both sharing their faith for the first time. People have shared Christ with servers at restaurants. They've told their coworkers about Jesus for the very first time.

What makes the message of this book so important for the church today? Let me suggest three reasons.

1. **It's simple.** You don't need a seminary education to do this. You can lead a person to faith in Christ

on one day, and that person is ready to share his or her faith on the very same day. If you have a pen and can find a piece of paper—or a napkin—you'll have everything you need.

2. **It's visual.** As you know, we live in an increasingly visual world. When you share your faith using the 3 Circles approach, you're engaging the ears and the eyes of the person with whom you're sharing.

3. **It's a great conversation transition.** The single greatest obstacle to getting church members to share their faith is their inability to transition the conversation to spiritual matters. We're around people all the time at ball games, on airplanes, and in lines in stores. This book teaches you to transition everyday conversations into gospel conversations simply by starting with the brokenness that's all around us.

For way too long, evangelism and missions have been seen as the exclusive responsibility of trained pastors. That's both unbiblical and dangerously unhelpful for the church today. Our mission field in North America is too vast and our message too urgent not to engage every single believer in our pursuit of the Great Commission.

Every Life on Mission Matters

To my parents—and ultimately our entire family—the on-mission life of Bill Sullivan mattered as much as any preacher they'd ever hear. Because God used him to share the good news about Jesus that night so many years ago, the entire trajectory of our family changed.

I pray this book will help the churches of North America discover this truth and mobilize a new generation of Bill Sullivans to invest their lives in everyday gospel conversations that will leave a ripple effect in the generations to come.

Kevin Ezell, president, North American Mission Board

Introduction

These are text messages we have received from people who attend Family Church:

> My wife and I shared the 3 Circles with a couple experiencing real brokenness last night. They both accepted Jesus as their Savior and decided to get baptized. They will be part of our missional community. Praise the Lord.

> I was able to share the gospel twice this morning—both received Christ and agreed to meet for follow-up discipleship. Praise God!

I shared the gospel with a lady sitting next to me on my flight to San Francisco. She was moved by the Spirit of God and believed. As I listened to her story, it was clear to me that God has been wooing her to Himself long before I even met her today. After believing and going through parts of the Bible with me, she borrowed my Bible and read 20+ chapters right away! I know it is our responsibility to point our newborn siblings in the right direction.

Hey! I just left a missional community training at church a little early so I could go home and share the gospel with my mother. She decided to repent and believe. My mother, stepfather, and I are going to begin reading the Bible together once a week. I don't even feel like this is actually happening. Please pray earnestly for me and my family, that we will be reproducing disciples.

Sorry to text you so late, but I showed my buddy the 3 Circles, and he wants to follow Jesus and get baptized. I couldn't wait till tomorrow to tell you. Sorry!! Have a good night!

I had the opportunity to share the 3 Circles this week with two people: one red light and one green light. With the green light, I made a copy of the first commandment Bible study you gave me, and we are studying it. Today I have a meeting scheduled at 10:00 a.m. to share the 3 Circles. God is doing amazing things!!!!

I just want to share with you what happened today. My wife left the meeting last night desiring to share the gospel. Today God opened the door, and this is the text I received from her: "I cannot contain my excitement . . . And to think that I was so nervous about it all. I shared the gospel with my coworker, and she said yes to Jesus." Tonight she is sharing the gospel with her husband and sister.

> I shared the 3 Circles with not one, but two girls. It was so super awesome. I was so afraid . . . God carried me through!

These are ordinary people who have seized the moment to turn everyday conversations into gospel conversations.

Broken World

We live in a broken world. You don't have to look far to realize it. In the United States, about 40 percent of children live in single-parent homes,[1] 40 percent of those have no contact with their fathers,[2] 33 percent of all Americans carry credit card debt,[3] and an estimated twenty million people are ensnared in some kind of addiction.[4] Top this with a 2014 Pew Research Center report revealing that 36 percent of millennials are now religious "nones"—people unaffiliated with any type of faith at all.[5]

We're the Humpty Dumpty nation. "Humpty Dumpty sat on the wall. Humpty Dumpty had a great fall. All the king's horses and all the king's men couldn't put Humpty together again." We've fallen, we're broken, and we can't figure out how to put all the pieces back together again. And it's not for a lack of trying. We all recognize what's wrong in our world today. We all have a sense of the brokenness, and we try our best to fix it. We teach values in the public schools. We attempt to provide health care for every individual. We study prison recidivism rates and implement behavior-modification programs to reduce them. There are all kinds of people trying all kinds of things to put our nation back together again. Fortunately for us, God has given us the solution.

God's answer to brokenness is this: repent and believe in Jesus. This gospel is how God puts broken people back together again. Once we repent and believe, God's Spirit helps us recover and pursue His design. God is the one who created the world and every human being in it. He's the one who knit us together in our mothers' wombs. He's the one who knows the plans He has for us.

His Word is our blueprint for living and teaches us how to steward our relationships, money, stress, and all of our broken pieces.

If God has put us back together, then He has also given us a job. He has tasked us with helping Him fix our broken world. God inspired Paul to give us this mandate in 2 Corinthians 5:17–21 (emphasis ours). This may be a familiar passage to us, but remember that it's written to a fledgling church full of new believers. They aren't seasoned believers. They haven't been to seminary. They actually get it wrong more than they get it right. As you read this passage, read it through that contextual lens:

> Therefore, if anyone is in Christ, he is a new
> creation; old things have passed away, and
> look, new things have come. Everything
> is from God, who *reconciled* us to Himself
> through Christ and gave us the ministry of
> *reconciliation*: That is, in Christ, God was
> *reconciling* the world to Himself, not count-
> ing their trespasses against them, and He has
> committed the message of *reconciliation* to us.

> Therefore, we are ambassadors for Christ,
> certain that God is appealing through us.
> We plead on Christ's behalf, "Be *reconciled* to
> God." He made the One who did not know
> sin to be sin for us, so that we might become
> the righteousness of God in Him.

As Paul instructs these new Christians, he uses some form of the word *reconciliation* five times to describe the work of the gospel in the life of repenting and believing Christians. The word *reconciliation* means to take things that have been broken apart and put them back together again. If only all the king's horses and all the king's men had heard the gospel!

The book you hold in your hands is a simple strategy to train new and seasoned believers to join God in His reconciliation work.

CHAPTER ONE

Our Mission Fields

When we were growing up, the church had a strategy, and it worked for a season. We believed in the church version of *Field of Dreams*—if we build it, they will come. We built bigger buildings and provided more and better programming. We attracted people to our churches, and many of them came.

This strategy works when people in our nation identify with church. After all, we were founded as one nation *under God*. For us, a clearer understanding of our missional context has motivated us to abandon this regional megachurch strategy. According to Gallup poll research, one-third of all Americans now consider themselves non-religious, saying that "religion is not an important part of their daily life and that they seldom or never attend religious services."[6] The Pew Research Center has reported a growing number of nones—people who don't identify with any faith tradition. Their most recent report cited a 6 percent increase in nones and an alarming 8 percent drop in the number of self-identifying Christians.[7] This is certainly true where we live. There are 1.4 million people living in Palm Beach County, Florida, and 96 percent of them are irreligious and unchurched.[8] In fact, West Palm Beach, Florida, ranks first on Barna Research Group's report ranking American cities by the percentage of residents who have never regularly attended church.[9]

Couple this with the fact that Americans are no longer motivated to go out of their way for many things, including church. We can access everything we want electronically from the comfort of our own homes. If you don't believe us, just consider the fate of the American shopping mall. No new enclosed malls have been built since 2006, and Robin Lewis, author of *The New Rules of Retail*, predicts fully half of all our malls will close in the next ten years.[10]

If we're going to reach the millions who have yet to hear the gospel, we need to rethink our current invite strategy. Since we aren't going to get them to "come and see" what we're doing, we need to figure out ways to take the good news to the places they live, work, and play.

When you think about it, this makes a lot of sense. Have you ever walked through the food court of a mall and been offered a free food sample? The restaurant giving out the free samples is hoping that one taste of their product will convince you to buy your own entrée. Imagine if instead of giving you the free sample, they gave you an invite card to come to a taste sampling four or five days away in another location. How many people would go to that trouble?

Yet this is the invite strategy many churches have adopted. In fact, we have often taken it further than that. If we can't motivate our people to hand out invite cards, we go ahead and do a direct-mail piece. We think that people will want to come and see what we have to offer. The ever-shrinking Christian population and changing U.S. trends demand that we reconsider this strategy. No clever social-media push, pithy sermon series, trendy worship style, or relevant programming is going to draw them in. Honestly, they could care less about all our bells and whistles, and most of them just aren't going to come.

We Need to See Multiplication

The task before us is massive. If we want to turn back lostness in North America, we need to stop talking about faster addition and start considering strategies for multiplication.

Our Family Church strategy is this: abandon the regional megachurch model and create a network of neighborhood churches. Our method is to mobilize disciples to make disciples who make disciples.

In the book of Acts, we see that the movement of the Holy Spirit spread like wildfire in the ancient world. Jesus commissioned the apostles, and within weeks there were already more than eight thousand new believers! Everybody was telling everybody. Churches were being planted left and right.

The apostles didn't have years of seminary or formal training under their belts, but they did have the power of the Holy Spirit and the things they had seen and heard. Our challenge is to take what we have seen and heard about Jesus and tell everybody—to multiply disciples by the thousands and millions.

It's not something we can do if we just leave it up to the "professionals." We have fifteen pastors on staff at our church and 1.4 million people to reach. This is an impossible task. We don't need fifteen pastors working harder and doing more to reach and disciple 1.4 million people. We need more like two hundred thousand people engaging in the mission to reach and disciple seven people each!

We're going to have to engage hundreds of thousands of people, and that means church will have to look different. It may not be church in a building with a full-time pastor and staff. It might be church in a store or a park or a home. If we do this, we can reach millions of people and plant thousands of churches.

Markers of a Multiplying Movement

As we began to reconsider our strategy and method, we started looking at emerging movements of new believers and new churches around the world. We found the following common characteristics among movements in China, Southeast Asia, India, and Africa:

- expanded vision
- focused prayer
- simple, reproducible gospeling tools
- abundant seed sowing
- frequent, intentional training
- rapid obedience
- generational discipleship
- loving accountability
- celebrating stories
- multiplying churches

Expanded Vision

Leaders in multiplying movements around the world are seeing God reconcile millions to Himself. They are committed to consistently keeping the big picture in front of people and connecting it with daily gospel responsibility. They continually urge believers to pursue the lost and relentlessly train believers to share the gospel.

Consider our context at Family Church. In order to move our county from 96 percent lost to 95 percent lost in one calendar year, we need to make fourteen thousand new disciples (1 percent of 1.4 million=14,000). Let that sink in for a minute. We were forced to ask whether the strategies that we now embrace enable us to reach this goal. Remember that we are merely considering a strategy to effect a 1-percent change. What about your mission field? How many new disciples would you need to reach to turn back the lostness in your immediate area just 1 percent? Churches across America need to begin having this conversation. We believe that if more churches would own a vision like this, then we could see a multiplying movement in America.

At our church, we have tried to bring the air war (vision and motivation) and ground war (strategy and training) together to keep this vision before our people. Our big idea: we want every resident of South Florida to have repeated opportunities to hear and respond to the gospel. Let's reach South Florida through the power of the gospel. We are committed to communicating it at every turn—every worship service, ministry event, new members class, leadership rally, staff meeting, training event, and meal with a church member. We regularly remind people that 96 percent of the people with whom they interact every day don't know or pursue God's design for their lives. Unless our church has ignored every word we've said, they know our vision is to plant one hundred neighborhood churches made up of people who have repented and who believe in Jesus.

Focused Prayer

God is reconciling the world to Himself. It's His work, and we have to trust Him to do it. Prayer aligns our hearts with God's heart for the lost. It helps us tune in to do God's work in God's way. Jesus said people only come to Him if the Father draws them (John 6:44). He says that we can ask for anything in His name, and He will do it (John 14:14). We know that praying for people's salvation is in His will because the Bible says that He doesn't want anyone to perish (2 Pet. 3:9).

We also know that as we set out to take Satan's territory from him, we're going into a battle zone. We aren't fighting against flesh and blood, but against the rulers of darkness and spiritual powers of evil (Eph. 6:12). Our weapons in this war, according to Ephesians 6, are the Word of God and prayer. Jonathan Edwards once said, "It is God's will through his wonderful grace, that the prayers of his saints should be one of the great principal means of carrying on the designs of Christ's kingdom in the world. When God has something very great to accomplish for his church, it is his will that there should precede it the extraordinary prayers of his people."[11] Focused prayer is an integral part of any sustainable multiplying movement.

We challenge people to make a personal list of the people they know who are far from God—family, friends, neighbors, coworkers, and so on. We intentionally and frequently pray for these individuals both corporately and privately. It is prayer that prepares their hearts—and ours—for everyday gospel conversations.

Simple, Reproducible Gospeling Tools

Movements that we studied have developed simple gospeling tools that are reproducible and reproducing. A reproducible gospeling tool is one that a new believer can easily grasp and share with others. A reproducing tool is one that multiplies disciples. Leaders in multiplying movements intentionally and repeatedly train believers in how to use these tools. If you've ever built something, you know the right tool is the key to getting the job done quickly and effectively. Each movement finds a set of tools that work in their context, and they stick with them.

People today are seeking relationships. They don't want to feel like they're projects. This is why we've developed a tool that is more relational. Our tool trains people to turn everyday conversations into gospel conversations. We'll discuss our 3 Circles conversation guide in chapter 5. Since we have released this tool, national and international organizations have embraced it for its ease of use and effectiveness. It is proving to be both reproducible and reproducing. We look forward to seeing what God will do as more and more ordinary people share the extraordinary power of the gospel using the 3 Circles.

Abundant Seed Sowing

"Now the One who provides seed for the sower and bread for food will provide and multiply your seed and increase the harvest of your righteousness" (2 Cor. 9:10). Multiplying movements recognize that the size of the harvest is directly connected to the amount of seed the sowers scatter. In fact, those who have been a part of multiplying movements say people need to "overseed." The gospel advances when people sow regularly and generously, not erratically and sparingly. This is why leaders of multiplying movements train new believers to go and immediately begin sharing the gospel. They also spend a considerable amount of time training existing believers to embrace and use reproducible gospeling tools. It's not the carefully placed seed that grows. The farmer doesn't need an advanced degree in horticulture to have an abundant harvest. He scatters the seed and then trusts God to water it and make it grow. Gospel seeds work the same way. Multiplying movement leaders are witnessing first-hand the hundredfold yield that Jesus told His disciples about in the parable of the sower (Luke 8:8).

We want every resident of Palm Beach County to have repeated opportunities to hear and respond to the gospel. We know we aren't going to see a multiplying movement until we see people repenting and believing *every day*. It's not enough to preach the gospel only on Sunday. It's not enough for a handful of seminary-trained individuals to tell several hundred people the good news once a week. We have to scatter more seed than that. We have to see everyday people scattering seed every day of the week. We need to oversow Palm Beach County and all of South Florida. Then—and only then—will a multiplying movement break out!

Frequent, Intentional Training

Think of anyone whom you respect for his or her accomplishments. Get a picture of that person in your mind. Tiger Woods? Harry Connick Jr.? Venus Williams? People who are really good at something practice frequently and intentionally. Multiplying movements are just as committed to training as any professional athlete. They think more like trainers than teachers. They practice, practice, practice, and then practice some more. A commitment to frequent, intentional training is the key factor that distinguishes a multiplying movement from one of fast addition.

Imagine that you entered a powerlifting competition scheduled to take place in six weeks. You could prepare by watching weight-lifting videos or going to several talks about weight lifting, or you could actually go to the gym and lift some weights. There you could increase weight and increase reps.

Malcolm Gladwell, in his book *Outliers: The Story of Success*, concludes that it takes ten thousand hours of practice before someone truly excels in his or her field. He isn't suggesting some magic formula for success but emphasizing the importance of repetition in any serious endeavor. What could be more important than excelling in the mission God gave us to go and make disciples?

We have to learn to think like trainers rather than teachers. People learn better by doing. We've stopped doing all the talking and started giving people opportunities to break into groups and practice with each other. We help them practice transitions, the 3 Circles, invitations, and responses. Our disciples are much better equipped the more reps they get during training. Once they're equipped, they can become trainers themselves.

Rapid Obedience

Multiplying movements embrace the biblical model of immediately commissioning new believers to share the gospel. In fact, new believers are an essential stimulus in multiplying movements. New believers go from converted to commissioned instantly using the principles found in 2 Corinthians 5:17–21. They can immediately create a list of people who are far from God and understand that they are the best ones to reach these people. Multiplying movements train new believers with a simple, reproducible gospeling tool and give them a set time by which to report on their gospel-sharing progress.

If we could have one do-over in our ministry, it would be to embrace more quickly this strategy of immediately training and releasing new believers. For too long, we told new believers that their first steps of obedience were to give, serve, and join a group. We moved them from converted to comfortable as quickly as possible. Now don't get us wrong—we believe in giving, serving, and being in a community. However, a new believer is uniquely positioned to go and tell others about this Jesus whom they just met. They know a lot of people who are far from God. Their lives haven't been all cleaned up, but they can tell the story just like the Samaritan woman at the well, who immediately went and told her whole town about Jesus (John 4:4–42).

Generational Discipleship

Paul writes to his young disciple Timothy and encourages him to train others as Paul had trained him. Paul casts a vision for Timothy, mentioning that these faithful men will then teach other reliable men (2 Tim. 2:2). This is an example of growth to the fourth generation:

Paul ➡ Timothy ➡ faithful men ➡ reliable men

A disciple is someone who has repented and believed in Jesus, been baptized, and joined Jesus' mission of making disciples through the local church. Multiplying movements equip people to be disciple makers by giving them the tools they need to share the gospel, baptize, and teach others to obey. Jesus commissioned us to "go and make disciples of all nations, baptizing them in the name of the Father and of the Son and of the Holy Spirit, and *teaching them to obey* everything I have commanded you" (Matt. 28:19–20a NIV, emphasis ours).

Multiplying movements worldwide are seeing generational discipleship go well beyond the fourth generation. Jeff Sundell, an IMB missionary who helped foster massive evangelistic movements in South Asia, says six streams of fourth-generation growth are one indicator of a verifiable multiplying movement. Multiplying movement leaders are constantly watching for—and reporting on—new movements.

We've worked hard to help our pastors, staff, and key leaders understand the vision and language of generational discipleship. This is a completely new conversation, vision, and measurement for us. We strategically placed generational maps (see the appendix) in meeting areas so that our staff and key leaders can frequently see

what we're talking about. Each week we give updates
on those whom we are discipling as well as those whom
they are discipling. We're looking for "supersowers" and
potential trainers. Ultimately, we're looking for streams
of fourth-generation growth. We're watching for a verifiable multiplying movement to break out. Our generational maps also help hold us accountable to each other
to do the work God has entrusted to us.

Loving Accountability

Multiplying movements love accountability. They
realize too much is at stake to leave to happenstance.
They set and review "go and grow" goals at each gathering. They ask, "With whom are you going to share the
gospel, and with whom are you going to share a spiritual principle you've learned?" Leaders of multiplying
movements believe that every disciple of Jesus must join
Jesus' reconciliation mission. They also believe every
follower of Jesus should be intentionally discipling at
least one person. These beliefs are reinforced with loving
accountability.

Accountability ensures that multiplication is more than just a pipe dream. True to our sinful human nature, all of us tend to drift away from God's mission. We get consumed with our own agendas. We're so busy with the cares of this world that the Word of God and the mission of God are no longer at the forefront of every day. The Bible says we are to "be concerned about one another in order to promote love and good works" (Heb. 10:24). Solomon, the wisest man ever to live, writes, "Iron sharpens iron, and one man sharpens another" (Prov. 27:17). If we're going to reenergize our efforts to make disciples, then we must hold each other accountable to live as everyday missionaries.

We incorporated accountability into our missional community structure. At each gathering, we report on our previous "go and grow" goals and share upcoming ones. This reporting idea is straight from the school of Jesus. In Luke 9:10, Jesus sent out His disciples and then asked them to report what happened upon their return. Accountability isn't meant to shame people; it's meant to further train and equip them. We can see where people get stuck and give them tools to make them more effective gospel-advancers. Again, we want to think like trainers or coaches who are helping people be more effective.

Celebrating Stories

It's important to take time to celebrate God's reconciling work. The spiritual battle for those actively engaged in advancing the gospel can be burdensome and difficult. This is why multiplying leaders look for opportunities to tell each other the wonderful things God is doing. They encourage one another with texts, e-mails, photos, phone calls, and gatherings.

These stories are also a great way to train and motivate others to keep sowing gospel seeds. They proclaim, "Yes! God is still reconciling the world to Himself." A wise trainer will use the power of story to cast vision for new and existing believers. Our natural drift is away from the Great Commission, which is why we need to be reminded regularly that God is at work and He wants us to join Him.

Every day we receive texts, calls, or e-mails from our church members. They love sharing with us how God is using them as they turn everyday conversations into gospel conversations using the 3 Circles. We have received and shared stories from eight-year-old children, newly saved drug addicts, teenagers at the beach, and longtime believers who have never before shared their faith. People who doubted the effectiveness of the tool have tried it and found it effective. Others who lacked confidence are now comfortable telling their friends. For us, celebrating these stories fuels our sense that God is up to something big. He really is rescuing people on a day-to-day basis like we see Him doing in the book of Acts. We all love a good story. What better story is there than that of people daily repenting and believing the gospel?

Multiplying Churches

When disciples multiply, new churches spring up—churches under trees, in schools, and in homes, and even churches in churches. They meet on different days of the week and have varying leadership structures. They are volunteer-led, bivocational, and run by full-time staff. The point is that these churches come in all shapes and sizes, but they hold some things in common. They constantly celebrate those coming to faith and being baptized. They then train these new believers and immediately deploy them as missionaries to go and tell others the gospel of Jesus. They multiply disciples until they can gather them into yet another community called church.

We actually need thousands of multiplying churches in South Florida. Our goal is to start one hundred of them. We've had hundreds of longtime church members leave their comfort zones to help launch new neighborhood churches. It's been amazing to see how many are willing to go. We have intentionally followed the biblical pattern of sending out our very best. We will keep telling people about the things we have "seen and heard."

Those are the key markers of multiplying movements, and the results speak for themselves:

- In Bhojpuri, India, between 50,000 and 83,000 believers were baptized in a twelve-month period.[12]
- A multiplying movement in Mongolia produced 60,000 new believers during the 1990s.[13]

- In 2001, Chinese house church leaders reported baptizing 500,000 people in a twelve-month period.[14]
- In an Asian Muslim country, more than 150,000 Muslims came to faith in Jesus from 1984 to 2004.[15]
- Cambodia has seen 60,000 new believers over the past ten years.[16]

The gospel is spreading like wildfire because God is reconciling the world to Himself. New believers worldwide are being equipped and challenged to immediately go and make disciples.

Our Goal: Every Resident

Paul had been asking God for an opportunity to go to Asia and proclaim the gospel. Acts 19:10 ESV tells how God answers Paul's prayers and reveals the effectiveness of his travels (Paul's third missionary journey): "This continued for two years, so that *all the residents* of Asia heard the word of the Lord, both Jews and Greeks."

The area they were reaching contained an estimated 8.2 million people.[17] Think about those phrases "continued for two years" and "all the residents." What if this were our goal? What if we asked God to help us reach all six million South Floridians (Palm Beach, Broward, and Miami-Dade counties)? What strategy could accomplish this in a two-year period? This is why we've tried to contextualize the ten markers of a multiplying movement. It's why we're striving to become not just gospel preachers, but gospel trainers. It's why we're committed to equipping everyday, ordinary people to be missionaries to the places they live, work, and play.

CHAPTER TWO

The Gospel

If our goal is to turn everyday conversations into gospel conversations, we need to be able to clearly articulate the gospel. This may seem like a no-brainer, but if we did a "man in the pew" survey, we would discover that most people couldn't clearly articulate the gospel.

Jimmy can recall how he learned this the hard way early on in his ministry. Here's his story:

> I knew God had called me to preach, and I was in seminary being trained for the pastorate when I went to the Philippines with one of my mentors, Bob Tebow. Bob took me

to a huge outdoor market on the island of
Mindanao and told me to preach the gospel.
And preach I did. I mean I really brought
it. A crowd gathered. People were engaged.
I told them about Jesus and the perfect life
He lived and the death He died. I explained
how He died on the cross for my sins and
their sins. I told them that if they repented
and believed in Jesus, God would forgive all
their sins. People responded. Approximately
a hundred people came out of that crowd that
day and professed faith in Jesus.

It was an amazing feeling! I was exhila-
rated and confident that I had done what
God called me to do—I preached the gospel.

Later that night I sat down with Bob to
review the day, and I was right. He thought
I had given a great effort. He told me he
was proud of me and that my passion really
showed. There was just one problem, he said:
I had failed to preach the gospel. He went
on to explain that I didn't tell the Filipinos

that Jesus rose from the dead. I preached
part of the gospel, but not the whole gospel.
Bob told me emphatically, "If you are going
to preach the gospel—preach *the* gospel." He
told me that I should never, ever evangelize
without presenting the death *and* resurrection of Jesus. I was embarrassed, but I've
never forgotten that lesson. I received excel-
lent training that day!

What Is the Gospel?

The apostle Paul gives us a complete and succinct
presentation of the gospel in 1 Corinthians 15:1–4:

> Now brothers, I want to clarify for you the
> gospel I proclaimed to you; you received
> it and have taken your stand on it. You are
> also saved by it, if you hold to the message I
> proclaimed to you—unless you believed for
> no purpose. For I passed on to you as most
> important what I also received: that Christ

died for our sins according to the Scriptures,
that He was buried, that He was raised on the
third day according to the Scriptures.

The gospel is simply this: Jesus died for our sins, He was buried, and God raised Him from the dead. It's His finished work that makes us right with God. Jesus did something for us that we could never do for ourselves.

Why This Is Good News

The word *gospel* literally means good news. It is good news that broken people like us can be in relationship with a righteous, perfect, holy, and just God. The truth is that God has a design for every area of our lives—our families, marriages, money, sex life, work life, and just plain life. God designed us to be in relationship with Him. He defines real life as knowing Him (John 17:21), but we have all departed from that design and gone our own way. The Bible calls this sin. We are born with a sinful nature, and sin comes naturally to us. There is no one who gets it right all of the time. We've all sinned and fallen short of God's perfect standard (Rom. 3:23).

This sin leaves us in brokenness. Brokenness is easy for most of us to understand. It looks like broken relationships, addiction, depression, discouragement, and shame. We all want out of brokenness, so we try to fix it. We medicate it with drugs or numb it with alcohol. We strive to be better people, hoping that somehow, someway, our good will outweigh our bad. We look for ways to alleviate our pain. When we do that, we just get more and more broken. This feels like a bad thing, but in many ways it's a good thing. It's the way God gets our attention. When we feel broken on the inside and everything is messed up, we know something needs to change. The Bible's word for change is *repent*.

Brokenness is what gets us ready to try God's solution for change: repent and believe the gospel. The change we really need comes from Jesus. God sent Jesus to live a perfect life, to die the death we deserve, and to be raised to life again, proving He is who He said He is and can do what He says He can do. Jesus came to forgive our sins. When we repent and believe in Him, He gives us supernatural power to recover and pursue God's design. Then Jesus sends us right back out into a broken world to tell other people how to find their way out of brokenness.

It doesn't matter what tool we use to tell others this good news. The tool can't save anybody; only the gospel can. What matters is that we include the essential information: Jesus died and was buried, and God raised Him from the dead. So whether we use the Four Spiritual Laws, the Roman Road, our own personal testimonies, or the 3 Circles, let's remember to tell the whole gospel. We love the gospel, not the tools.

Unpack the Gospel

Once we *experience* the gospel, we really don't have to *know* more about it to be qualified to explain it. However, let's take some time to unpack this life-changing truth.

Jesus

First of all, who is this Jesus? Jesus is God's one and only Son. He was conceived by the Holy Spirit and born of a woman—a virgin—as described in Matthew 1:18–23 (emphasis ours):

> The birth of Jesus Christ came about this way: After his mother Mary had been engaged to Joseph, it was discovered before they came together that *she was pregnant by the Holy Spirit*. So her husband Joseph, being a righteous man, and not wanting to disgrace her publicly, decided to divorce her secretly. But after he had considered these things, an angel of the Lord suddenly appeared to him in a dream, saying, "Joseph, son of David, don't be afraid to take Mary as your wife, because *what has been conceived in her is by the Holy Spirit*. She will give birth to a son, and you are to name Him Jesus, because He will save His people from their sins." Now all this took place to fulfill what was spoken by the Lord through the prophet: "See, the virgin will become pregnant and give birth to a son,

and they will name Him Immanuel," which is translated, "God is with us."

Jesus is God. This is difficult for us to comprehend. He is both God and God's Son. In our time- and space-contained reality, a father comes before a son. Not so with Jesus. He is coeternal with the Father and the Spirit. He has no beginning and no end. He has always been. The apostle Paul explains, saying, "He is the image of the invisible God, the firstborn over all creation. For everything was created by Him, in heaven and on earth, the visible and the invisible, whether thrones or dominions or rulers or authorities—all things have been created through Him and for Him" (Col. 1:15–16).

Jesus is fully God. He is all knowing, all powerful, and in all places at all times. He is coequal with God the Father and God the Spirit. There is no hierarchy in the Trinity. There is order and submission, but there is equality.

Jesus is God with us. The Bible says that He didn't consider His equal position as God something to be grasped, but He emptied Himself and became one of us

(Phil. 2:6–7). He took on human flesh and lived life just like us. He got tired, hungry, thirsty, sad, and happy. He was—and is—a real person, just like us.

There is one major distinction between Jesus and other humans: Jesus never sinned—not one time. He knows what it's like to be tempted to sin. He was tempted in every way that we are, but He never sinned (Heb. 4:15). He was tempted to lie but didn't. He was tempted to look on a woman with lust but didn't. He was tempted to want things that weren't His but didn't. This is how He is able to help us in our times of need (Heb. 4:16). It's also what qualifies Him to do the work the Father sent Him to do.

Jesus Died for Our Sins

Jesus, who knew no sin, became sin for us (2 Cor. 5:21). God cannot mar His perfect design with broken people. This is why He fashioned a miraculous exchange. When Jesus died on the cross, God the Father took all of our sin, shame, and guilt and put it on Jesus. Then He took all of Jesus' righteousness and put it on those who repent and believe. Jesus died the death of a sinner so that believers can live as righteous people.

God set this plan in motion long before Jesus came down to Earth. He revealed it at the dawn of Creation when He covered Adam and Eve's sin with animal skins (Gen. 3:21). It was then that God established the shedding of blood as His method for covering sin. He spelled it out in His law, saying, "For the life of a creature is in the blood, and I have appointed it to you to make atonement on the altar for your lives, since it is the lifeblood that makes atonement" (Lev. 17:11). There is no forgiveness of sin without it (Heb. 9:22).

The law emphasized the shedding of innocent blood. God's holiness requires the blood of a lamb without blemish (Exod. 12:5). This is why it's important for us to understand the essence of Jesus. He is a sinless man, and it's only His blood that could cover our sin once and for all (Heb. 10:10). Jesus died for our sins so we can receive this free gift of life forever in God's perfect presence.

He Was Buried

Jesus didn't swoon. His body wasn't stolen. He was really dead, and they really buried Him. When the Roman soldiers pierced His side, one eyewitness testified that water and blood flowed out (John 19:34). This is real, physical evidence that Jesus died—gave up His life—so that we might live.[18]

Then they took His body from the cross and laid it in a borrowed tomb. The tomb was sealed with a massive stone and the emperor's signet. Elite Roman soldiers guarded it. If the body had been stolen, there would have been plenty of evidence and plenty of eyewitnesses.

Jesus was definitely dead. "For the wages of sin is death" (Rom. 6:23). He took the death penalty we deserve. It's not a hoax or a trick, and what happened next is the lynchpin of the hope we have in Him.

God Raised Him from the Dead

Can you believe I (Jimmy) forgot this part that day in the Philippines? This is the best part. It's proof that Jesus is who He claimed to be and will deliver on His promise of eternal life. There were plenty of eyewitnesses to this event. "He appeared to Cephas, then to the Twelve. Then He appeared to more than five hundred brothers at one time; most of them are still alive, but some have fallen asleep. Then He appeared to James, then to all the apostles. Last of all, as to one abnormally born, He also appeared to me" (1 Cor. 15:5–8). When Paul recorded those words, a fact checker could have gone and found almost five hundred people who would say, "Yes, I saw Jesus die on the cross. I saw them seal Him in the tomb. And then, three days later, I saw Him walking around the city!"

Jesus isn't dead. He is alive. This makes Him unique among all religious figures. Buddha was alive. He was Siddharta Gautama, son of Suddhodana, the head of the Sakya tribe, and a member of the clan of Gautama. He was born in Nepal, and when he was twenty-nine years old, he set off on a spiritual journey of self-denial and contemplation. Buddha lived an exemplary life, and then he died. And he stayed dead.

Muhammad was also alive. He was born in AD 570 in the Arabian city of Mecca. He claimed to have received his first revelation from God when he was forty years old. He wrote his special revelations down in what we now know as the Koran. Muhammad lived a very religious life, but when he was sixty-three years old, he died. And he stayed dead.

Hinduism has a plurality of gods. In 1966, Swami Prabhupada started an American Neo-Hindu movement called the Hare Krishnas. His teaching propagated the achievement of a higher spiritual state known as Krishna Consciousness. Prabhupada was still striving to attain this pure state of mind in 1977 when he died. And he stayed dead.

Jesus also died. But He did not stay dead. Jesus is alive, seated in the heavenly realms with His Father. He will return one day to judge the living and the dead. He will judge based on the answer to this question alone: "Who do you say that I am?" (Matt. 16:15). God says, "The one who has the Son has life. The one who doesn't have the Son of God does not have life" (1 John 5:12). "Having" Jesus means believing He died for our sins, was buried, and was raised again.

Preach the Gospel

These are the essentials of the gospel, and we must clearly communicate them. Recently a well-known speaker gave a great talk to a large crowd. He was eloquent and emotional. His message moved people to respond. At the end of his talk, many people came forward to "give their lives to Jesus." All of these people responded, but the speaker had not articulated the gospel. He talked about Jesus, His promises to us, and the love, joy, peace, and strength He brings into our lives. But He didn't tell them how Jesus died for their sins and was buried, and how God raised Him from the dead.

We don't know what the Spirit of God did in that room. There may have been people with previous knowledge of Jesus' death for their sins, burial, and resurrection who truly believed that day. However, we must remember that eloquence and emotion are never substitutes for the gospel. The apostle Paul called the gospel "God's power for salvation" (Rom. 1:16). He also made this observation about his own preaching in 1 Corinthians 2:3–5: "I came to you in weakness, in fear, and much trembling. My speech and my proclamation were not with persuasive words of wisdom but with a powerful demonstration by the Spirit, so that your faith might not be based on men's wisdom but on God's power." The preacher that day could have used some training from Bob Tebow: "If you are going to preach the gospel—preach *the* gospel."

When we have gospel conversations, God draws people to His Son so that they will believe and have life. We want to share this simple, powerful, and extremely good news with every resident of South Florida. Will you commit to sharing it with every resident in your mission fields?

CHAPTER THREE

Everyday People and Conversations

Everyday People

When we were growing up, missionaries would come from time to time to visit our churches. They brought pictures and told stories of faraway people in faraway lands. It all seemed very exotic. It made people think, *I love Jesus, but I'm not sure I want to be a missionary.* Since then we've learned that we're all missionaries to the places where we currently live, work, and play. How many in our immediate area have never heard the good news that Jesus died for their sins and was buried, and that God raised Him from the dead? Who is going to tell them? Every believer needs to see himself or herself as a missionary. In short, we have to redefine the word "missionary" in our churches.

Most people in our churches feel unqualified and ill prepared to tell people about Jesus. They can list all of the reasons why someone else is better suited for the mission. George Stott, a nineteenth-century missionary to China, served faithfully despite only having one leg. When asked why he, with only one leg, should think of going to China, his remark was, "I do not see those with two legs going, so I must."[19]

Imagine if we truly embraced the Great Commission and trained believers to take the gospel to a broken world in spite of our limitations and inadequacies. Imagine what it would look like if those who sat in the pew on Sunday were intentionally sowing gospel seeds all week. Imagine if the average believer were trained to turn everyday conversations into gospel conversations.

Everyday Conversations

The average person has twenty-seven conversations per day.[20] A recent study revealed that both men and women utter an average of about sixteen thousand words each day.[21] We can talk about sports, weather, clothes, shoes, movies, and TV shows. We're even willing to debate the nuances of politics, the intricacies of health issues, or the complexities of national economic matters. However, when it comes to bringing up the simple gospel, we shy away. We break out in hives, our palms sweat, our tongues are tied, and we find ourselves talking about everything *but* the gospel. The idea of injecting Jesus into our conversations causes great anxiety and fear for ordinary believers and pastors alike.

Many believers are afraid that gospel conversations will be confrontational or argumentative. We think we have to be trained for every possible theological perspective we may encounter before we can share the gospel. We're often overwhelmed by the need to memorize a dozen verses or anxious that someone might ask a question we can't answer. Sadly, sharing the gospel has lost its simplicity. It doesn't have to be this way.

Consider the natural flow of everyday conversations. Our conversations include laughter, introspection, empathy, and body language. We speak and we listen. Ultimately, our conversations have an introduction, a general direction, and a conclusion. Our conversations are never completely random or altogether open-ended. People are often looking to us to offer meaningful responses.

When was the last time you had a conversation and the person with whom you were talking shared a problem, issue, or concern? It happens a lot. These interactions are gospel opportunities, and we train people to recognize and seize them.

Here's a message we got recently:

Today I stopped to get coffee, and the guy at the table next to me started a conversation with me, and it happened just like you said. He shared a problem, I asked if I could share something with him, and he said yes. He was so moved by our conversation that he took the napkin I shared the gospel on and went straight home to share with his wife. AMAZING.

There you go! An everyday conversation turned into a gospel conversation that ended with a man crossing from death to life. Also, notice his immediate willingness to go and tell someone else. Every day is filled with opportunities like this one that will never again be captured. If we miss them, they're gone. When we're willing to turn conversations to the gospel, we'll find that the gospel *is* robust. God is *still* reconciling the world to Himself. "Surely the arm of the LORD is not too short to save, nor his ear too dull to hear" (Isa. 59:1 NIV).

Let the Gospel Be the Filter

Eddie and Jacob are two young men who were holding each other accountable to share the gospel intentionally. They had been praying together for open doors and opportunities to do so. One day, while walking through the grocery store, they saw a man and quickly assumed that he probably wouldn't be open to a gospel conversation. He was a biker type: tattoos, leather vest, ponytail—the whole nine yards. Eddie and Jacob decided they would go ahead and approach the man despite their initial evaluation. To their surprise, he was very open to the gospel because his wife had been diagnosed with cancer only days earlier. The gospel gave this man great hope in the midst of his trial, and he repented and believed.

Another church member was sitting in a hospital waiting room with only one other man. The man was somewhat unkempt and seemed irritated and unapproachable. Plus, the man's size was a bit intimidating: he looked fully capable of hurting anyone who bothered him. Our church member prayed for the man and thought about God's arms not being too short to save. Then he mustered up his courage and spoke to the man, saying, "Sir, I know you don't know me, but I'd like to share some good news with you." The man responded by saying he "sure could use some good news." He came over and sat next to the church member, who shared the gospel with him using the 3 Circles. The man repented and believed in Jesus right there in that hospital waiting room.

Here's a list of the least-likely people to repent and believe the gospel:

- Paul, who persecuted the church and killed Christians to stop the spread of the gospel (Acts 8:1).
- the man possessed by demons (Mark 5:1–15).
- the woman caught in adultery (John 8:1–11).
- the thief on the cross (Luke 23:32–43).

There is often a scriptural paradox regarding those who followed Jesus and those who rejected Him. The people who we think would follow Jesus don't (e.g., religious leaders, those who studied Scripture, rich young rulers, etc.). The people who we think would never come to Jesus do (e.g., tax collectors, thieves, prostitutes, murderers, etc.).

How do we know when someone is ready to hear and genuinely respond to the gospel? The fact is we really never know what God is doing in someone's heart. We need to have frequent, intentional gospel conversations and then allow the gospel to be the filter.

Connecting the Dots

Here's our simple, reproducible method for turning everyday conversations into gospel conversations:

Everyday conversation
(problem, issue, or concern)

↓

transition

↓

gospeling tool (3 Circles)

↓

invitation and response

↓

train new disciple (rapid obedience)

Before ascending to heaven, the resurrected Jesus gave His followers the charge to go and make disciples. The book of Acts is Luke's record of how they did just that. Their gospel conversations fueled the first Christian multiplying movement. International Mission Board President, David Platt, while speaking at Family Church, said, "What fueled the exponential and explosive growth of Christianity in the first century was how ordinary people spoke of the gospel to everyone they knew. They didn't need seminary degrees, denominational backing, or all the answers. These early believers had gospel conversations every day."

Here are just a few examples of those gospel conversations:

- Peter used many words to bear witness and exhort his listeners to repent and believe the gospel (Acts 2:40).
- Early believers shared the gospel, and the Lord added to their number daily those who were being saved (Acts 2:47).

- A beggar asked for money, and John and Peter transitioned the conversation to the gospel (Acts 3).
- The number of disciples rapidly increased as ordinary men shared the word of God (Acts 6).
- When persecution came, Christians went out and shared the word of the Lord (Acts 8:4).
- An angel of the Lord told Philip to head south toward Gaza, and on his way, he met an Ethiopian who couldn't understand the Scripture he was reading. This conversation ended with the man believing the gospel and being baptized (Acts 8:26–40).
- A newly converted Paul was discipled by a believer named Ananias, and the church spread and increased in number (Acts 9:31).

On and on it goes. By Acts 17, Jason and other believers are dragged to the city authorities and labeled as men "who have turned the world upside down" (Acts 17:6).

These new believers didn't get that label by telling people the gospel once or twice a year. They intentionally seized every opportunity God gave them to proclaim the good news. This is the means to the end of having every resident in your region hear the gospel (Acts 19:10).

Let the Training Begin

Do you ever have conversations with other people? Do people ever share problems, issues, or concerns with you? The next few chapters will take us through the process of turning everyday conversations into gospel conversations. Please read, study, and practice them with a group of believers so that you fully grasp the concepts, strategies, and results. Other people's perspectives, struggles, and victories will help develop strategies that might lead to a multiplying movement where you live. Can you imagine thousands upon thousands of people in your community repenting and believing the gospel? Can you imagine God using you as part of this plan? We hope you can, because God is using us to reconcile the world to Himself.

CHAPTER FOUR

Transition To The Gospel

Have you ever been stuck? People get stuck all of the time. We get stuck in the mud, on an icy road, on math problems, in a relationship, or in besetting sin. As we write, our entire country is under winter weather advisories. Every news station is showing footage of stranded cars, trucks, planes, and trains. People can't get where they want to go, and they need help. Sometimes this is how believers get when it comes to having everyday gospel conversations. They know where they want to go, but they can't get there.

Think back over your last five or six face-to-face conversations. In any of these conversations, did someone share a problem, issue, or concern with you? Chances are they did. So the real question is, how do we transition these everyday conversations to gospel conversations?

Transitioning conversations is actually something we do every day. We often change the course of a conversation with a question or a statement. Yet when it comes to transitioning to the gospel, we can think of a million reasons why we shouldn't do it. It will be awkward. The person may be offended. We might not be able to answer all of his or her questions. These doubts and fears seem small in comparison with those of people who literally put their lives on the line when they talk about Jesus. Nonetheless, they are still real fears to be conquered. This is why it's important to practice transitioning our conversations to the gospel.

Pray

This is one of our markers. We have to mention it again because sharing the gospel always starts with prayer. In the Old Testament book of Nehemiah, Nehemiah is an exile living in the Persian king's palace. He's a Jew who has been elevated to the most trusted—and dangerous—position. He's the cupbearer to the king, which means he drinks from the king's cup to make sure it isn't poisoned. When Nehemiah hears that his people and his city are in a state of brokenness, he is deeply troubled. Nehemiah 1:4–11 tells us that he fasts, mourns, and fervently prays for four months. Then when the opportunity arises, he shoots up a quick prayer and asks the king for permission and provision for God's rebuilding work (Neh. 2:4). The circumstance is unique, but the prayer principles are clear. We need to pray fervently for opportunities to address brokenness. Then when they come, we shoot off a quick prayer and seize the moment, trusting God to give us the words to say.

Listen

Jesus was sensitive to His surroundings. We know this by the incredible ways Jesus responded in each situation. He also used questions to transition the situation to the gospel.

When Jesus met a Samaritan woman at the well, He engaged her in conversation by asking, "Will you give me a drink?" (John 4:7 NIV). He then turned the conversation to the gospel, revealing that He is the source of eternal life.

When Jesus encountered a rich, young ruler, He asked him, "Why do you ask Me about what is good?" (Matt. 19:17). He knew the man was rich in good deeds but unwilling to accept the free gift of salvation. Jesus' question got to the heart of the matter.

When Jesus met an invalid lying by a healing pool, He engaged him with a question: "Do you want to get well?" (John 5:6). He then worked two miracles—He healed him physically and then forgave all his sins.

When the prostitute fell on Jesus' feet at the house of a religious leader named Simon, Jesus once again turned the conversation toward the gospel. As Simon doubted that Jesus really was a prophet, Jesus told him a story about two men who owed debts. One man owed a very large debt and the other a relatively small debt. And then He asked a question about the man who forgave the debt. Jesus asked Simon, "So, which of them will love him more?" (Luke 7:42). This drove the conversation to the heart of the gospel. Jesus ultimately said to Simon, "Therefore I tell you, her many sins have been forgiven; that's why she loved much" (Luke 7:47).

Jesus didn't respond to every situation in exactly the same way. Of course, He did have the benefit of being God. But we know that the Spirit of Jesus lives in believers, and this same Spirit helps us discern what to say and how to say it in every given situation.

Wait for It

We want to be people who are genuine, empathetic, and winsome. These characteristics come more easily to some than others. As we pray and ask God to give us opportunities, He will continually transform us. We also need to be open with others. We need to share with them our problems, issues, and concerns so that they will be comfortable sharing theirs with us. We do this because we really care about them. We don't want to come across as if we have an uncaring personal agenda; we want to be like Jesus. Jesus interacted on a human level in a way that attracted others to Him. Jesus is always willing to meet people where they are, but He never leaves them there. He addresses their emotional and physical needs but always delves into the spiritual too.

People don't want to be talked down to or have something shoved down their throats. Yet they rarely get angry or upset with honest, sincere, and helpful input, especially from someone they respect. This approach is predicated on relationship. It's not that gospel interactions will never happen between strangers, but they are certainly more likely to happen between friends. People typically share their problems, issues, or concerns with us when they trust us and think we have helpful insight. And they're right. After all, we've been entrusted with the ministry of reconciliation (2 Cor. 5:17–21). Christians have an eternal, spiritual perspective that people aren't going to get anywhere else.

We train believers to wait for that moment in the conversation when someone shares a problem, issue, or concern. This gives them an opening to tell that person the best news they will ever hear. Problems, issues, or concerns include disease, divorce, disappointment, and death. They involve parenting, marriage, work, money, and cancer. These topics drive our conversations almost daily, and a good transition can turn them from everyday conversations into gospel conversations.

So how do we get from problems, issues, and concerns to the gospel?

Transition Statement

A good transition statement is the key. We're going to give you an example, but remember that you have to develop a transition statement that works for you. We want you to develop *and* practice your transition. Again, if we're willing to practice the piano, our golf swing, or getting better at Clash of Clans, why shouldn't we practice transitioning to gospel conversations? We encourage people to practice transitioning a lot!

Here's our example: "I haven't been through the exact situation that you just mentioned, but I have had similar problems (or issues or concerns). Can I share something with you that has really helped me?"

Read that transition out loud.

Is it comfortable for you?

If not, write your own transition statement here:

_____

_____

_____

Read what you wrote out loud.

Now practice your transition. You can practice with a friend. You can have your small group practice with one another. Couples can practice. Families can practice. At our church, we practice at staff meetings and in small groups. Our Kids Ministry leaders have the kids practice. Practice really does make perfect. This is how we get more comfortable transitioning everyday conversations to gospel conversations.

Getting Unstuck

God is reconciling people right now and right where we live. Gospel multiplication isn't a relic of biblical days gone by. It isn't exclusive to movements in China, Southeast Asia, India, or Africa. It can happen in our communities if we can help believers get unstuck when it comes to sharing the gospel. Sometimes the desire is there, but they just need the right tools.

In the New Testament, the word *proclaim* is used more than seventy times. New Testament believers proclaimed as they went along their way, in homes, in the public square, and in the synagogues. It's clear that gospel proclamation wasn't confined to a weekly church service. Again, the book of Acts tells us how people repented and believed daily, and the number of new disciples multiplied greatly. Acts 9:31 tells us that as the church was being built up in Judea, Galilee, and Samaria. It multiplied.

The way Jesus trained His disciples is carefully chronicled in the Gospels. Jesus modeled for them that His mission was to the sick, lost, and broken. He cast the vision that the harvest was plentiful and in need of laborers. He sent them out, and they reported back. Once He received their report, "He took them along and withdrew privately to a town called Bethsaida" (Luke 9:10). Jesus often did some private schooling with His disciples. Both Jesus' example and the practical advice of Paul's letters tell us that it is our job to train and equip others:

- "A disciple is not above his teacher, but everyone who is fully trained will be like his teacher" (Luke 6:40).

- "And He personally gave some to be apostles, some prophets, some evangelists, some pastors and teachers, for the training of the saints in the work of ministry, to build up the body of Christ" (Eph. 4:11–12).

- "If you point these things out to the brothers, you will be a good servant of Christ Jesus, nourished by the words of the faith and the good teaching that you have followed" (1 Tim. 4:6).

- "All Scripture is inspired by God and is profitable for teaching, for rebuking, for correcting, for training in righteousness, so that the man of God may be complete, equipped for every good work" (2 Tim. 3:16–17).

When someone shares a problem, issue, or concern with us, we can pull out our well-practiced transition statements and see what happens. They may or may not lower the bridge and open a way for us to share the gospel. If at first we don't succeed, we try and try again. We learn from our mistakes and learn how to turn everyday conversations into gospel conversations.

CHAPTER FIVE

3 Circles Gospeling Tool

Two of the markers of multiplying movements are simple, reproducible gospeling tools and generational discipleship. The 3 Circles is proving effective in both areas. Recently we received a text message from a man who is new to our church. Until he joined Family Church, he had never heard of the 3 Circles, and he was quick to begin using it. His message read, "Pastor, Kyle [his disciple] led Rob to Christ, who led Steve to Christ, who led Anthony to Christ. Each person brought the next person to Christ via the 3 Circles, and each is continuing to be trained and discipled. If my math is right, we have made it to the fifth generation."

The 3 Circles[22] is a tool that works in our missional context. People in our broken world are looking for answers, and God has equipped us to give them.

It's Simple

The 3 Circles is *really* simple. It involves three circles connected by three arrows.

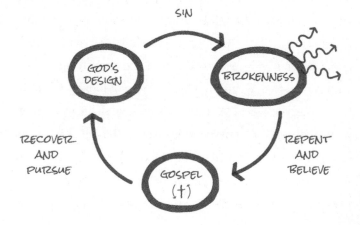

It begins with God's design. It follows an easily relatable script of every man, woman, and child's departure from God's design as sinful people that leads us all to brokenness. When something is broken, we try to fix it. Everyone wants out of brokenness. Ultimately our relief from brokenness is found in repentance and faith. We must repent and believe the gospel in order to be rescued from brokenness. The gospel is Christ dying in our place on the cross and taking the penalty that we deserve for our sins. He was resurrected, and in turn we are resurrected into a new life when we believe the gospel. Through God's grace we are able to recover and pursue His design for our lives—from whatever place of brokenness we find ourselves in.

The concept of recovering and pursuing God's design is crucial. Becoming a Christian doesn't get rid of our past mistakes or automatically fix the pain and consequences that resulted. The 3 Circles helps us understand God's saving and sanctifying work. New disciples understand that Christ's followers are lifelong repenters who need to rehearse the gospel daily. As believers, we continually depart from God's design. Every time we sin and find ourselves in brokenness, we should repent and remind ourselves of the power of the gospel. The 3 Circles allows those who are far from God to see the beauty of the gospel and equips believers to share it with others daily.

3 Circles Sample "Script"

Here is a simple script illustrating how the 3 Circles can center a conversation on the gospel. Imagine that two coworkers go to lunch—one is a disciple of Jesus, and one is far from God. The disciple knows that she has been given the ministry of reconciliation and that God is making His appeal to her coworkers through her. She has built a relationship with this work friend. She has been praying for her and asking God to give her the right opportunity to share the gospel as well as the boldness to seize that opportunity. The scene may play out like this:

PROBLEM, ISSUE, OR CONCERN

Work friend: I'm just struggling right now. Things aren't that great at home. My husband and I have totally different philosophies about how to raise our kids, and it's causing a lot of arguments and frustration. I don't feel loved or supported by my husband, and sometimes I wonder if it's even worth it.

TRANSITION

Christian: Thank you so much for sharing your parenting/marriage issues. I haven't had the exact same problem, but I've definitely experienced similar problems. Can I share something with you that has really helped me?

GOSPEL

She takes out a pen, grabs the napkin, draws a circle, and writes "God's design" in it.

Christian: I believe God has a design for our lives. We see God's design all around us: in the beauty of creation—a golden sunrise or a pink sunset—and in our own amazing bodies. The Bible says God knit us together in our mothers' wombs (Psalm 139). Knitting is delicate and intimate work, so we know that God personally designed us and has a purpose for our lives.

Now, I have to tell you that, although I knew of God's wonderful design early in life, I didn't always accept it or appreciate it. Honestly, I rebelled against it. I didn't want to be under anyone's design or rule. I wanted to go my own way, be my own boss, make my own decisions, and do things the way I wanted them done. I basically decided to depart from God's design.

She draws an arrow leading away from God's design.

Christian: The Bible has a word for this departure from God's design—the word is "sin." The Bible actually says that all have sinned and departed from God's design.

She writes the word "sin" next to the line.

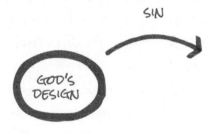

She then draws another circle and writes the word "bro-kenness" in it and draws some squiggly lines leading away from it.

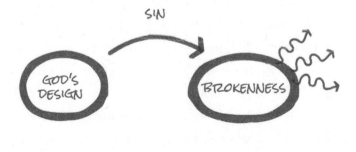

Christian: Unfortunately, our sin takes us all to a place of brokenness. Brokenness could look like struggling relationships, addiction, isolation, or despair. It's guilty feelings, shame, and emptiness. It's how we feel when we realize we've been used, or that we've used someone else. In fact, our whole world is broken. We see evidence of this everywhere—in every crime, in sickness, and even in death. These all are results of sin. We live in a broken world, and no one in this world is untouched by brokenness, but no one likes brokenness or wants to stay in it. If it's broken, we want to fix it. There are entire industries built around getting people out of brokenness. There are counseling centers, self-help books, afternoon TV shows, treatment centers, and many more. We do our best to fix our brokenness.

Some people try to numb their pain with drugs or alcohol. Others think the cure is another relationship. Some try to ramp up their personal discipline and dedication. Knowing they got themselves into brokenness, they think they can get themselves out. Some even turn to church or religion. We realize that something needs to change. But often, when we try to change ourselves, we

realize that the change we need has to come from some-
where else. Our attempts to fix our brokenness usually
only result in more brokenness.

*She draws the third circle and writes the word "gospel" in
it along with a down arrow, a cross, and an up arrow.*

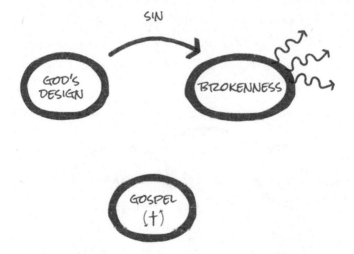

Christian: The word *gospel* means "good news." The
good news is that God sent His Son, Jesus, to live a perfect life (down arrow), die the death we deserve because
of our sin (cross), and be raised from the dead (up arrow).

The Bible says that when Jesus died on the cross, God did a miracle. He took all of our sin and put it on Jesus, and then He took all of Jesus' righteousness and put it on anyone who believes in Jesus. This means that we are no longer broken in God's eyes. We are made right with Him. All we have to do to get this right standing with God is repent and believe in Jesus.

She draws a second arrow away from brokenness pointing toward the gospel circle and writes "repent and believe."

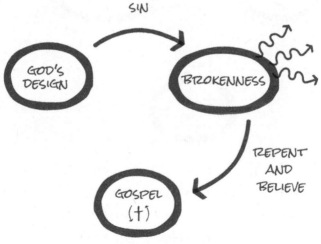

Christian: The change we really need comes through the gospel. The word *repent* means a change of mind that's followed by a change in direction. It means we were headed one way, trying to fix our own brokenness, and now we have turned from that and turned to Jesus. "Believe" means that we trust that Jesus' death, burial, and resurrection are what make us right with God. We believe it as much as we believe that the chairs we sit in are going to hold us up. Jesus Himself told people to "repent and believe in the good news!"—the gospel (Mark 1:15).

She draws the last arrow from gospel back toward God's design and writes the words "recover and pursue."

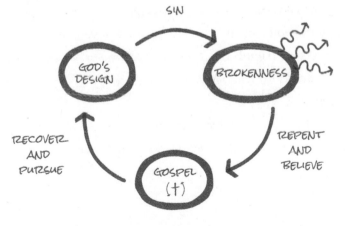

Once we repent and believe, we can begin to recover and pursue God's design. We get a do-over. Everybody loves a do-over. If we don't get it right the first time, we get to try again. God gives unlimited do-overs. None of us is perfect. Even if we have believed in Jesus and been made whole in God's eyes, we will still mess up. Repenting and believing doesn't fix everything, but it does forgive everything. Plus, we have Jesus helping us and walking with us. He changes our hearts and motivates us to recover and pursue God's design.

She shows the finished diagram to her work friend.

INVITATION

Christian: Does this diagram make any sense to you? As you look at it, where do you see yourself?

Work friend: *She points to "brokenness" and explains that she sees her marriage—and therefore, her life—as broken right now.*

Christian: Is there anything that would prevent you from repenting and believing the gospel today?

We will deal with responses to this invitation in the next chapter, but first let's cover a few important points about the 3 Circles.

Things to Remember

- **The 3 Circles is simply a tool.** We love and are committed to Christ, not tools. We always have to remember that this is God's work, and He's doing it. He is the one reconciling the world to Himself, and He just uses us as His mouthpieces.

- **It's your "napkin."** Each person can customize the 3 Circles to his or her own style. You can use more verses or less. You can use different verses. You can explain God's design in a different way. This is an open-source tool—make it your own.

- **Practice is key.** We take every opportunity to get people to practice the 3 Circles. When we have a meeting, a lunch, or a class, we take a few minutes to let the person or people practice the 3 Circles. If you're in a group, you can have them pair off and practice. If you're reading this book, and your spouse or child is nearby, put the book down and practice the 3 Circles.

- **Testimonies are essential.** The 3 Circles is a great training tool for helping believers articulate their testimony and their ability to share it with others.

Wildfire

In the book of Acts, the gospel spread like wildfire. There were no denominations, seminaries, TV preachers, Christian books, or gospel tracts. There were just ordinary people, extraordinary power, earnest prayer, and frequent gospel conversations. First-century Christians found the gospel robust as they told it to others daily. There was no power on earth that would stop them from sharing the good news that Jesus died for their sins, was buried, and God raised Him from the dead. They were put in prison, beaten, exiled, and martyred because they refused to stop telling people about Jesus.

The Bible makes this incredible statement about people who witnessed Jesus' disciples: "When they observed the boldness of Peter and John and realized that they were uneducated and untrained men, they were amazed and recognized that they had been with Jesus" (Acts 4:13). Uneducated, common people turned the world upside down.

This same fire has spread the gospel from Peter's first sermon in Acts 2 until today. It's ordinary people filled with the extraordinary power of God's Spirit who obey Jesus' command to *go* and make disciples. We are not ashamed of the gospel because we know it's the power of God for salvation (Rom. 1:16).

Each one of us has been entrusted with a very brief period of time in which to do God's reconciling work. The Bible uses words like "mist" (James 4:14 ESV) to describe the length of our days on this earth. If God has rescued and redeemed us out of our brokenness, He has left us here to show others the way. This is our time—let's seize our moments and make them count for all of eternity. Let's turn everyday conversations into conversations about Jesus. He was crucified for our sins and raised from the dead so that we could be rescued out of brokenness and live according to His design.

CHAPTER SIX

Invitation and Responses

Everyone likes to be invited. Even if we can't go, it's always nice to be asked. As children, we loved being invited to birthday parties. As we got a little older, it was an honor to be invited to special events. Great attention and expense go into every wedding invitation. In the Gospels we see God, through Jesus, give the most amazing invitation of all. God invites us to be reconciled to Him and spend eternity celebrating His goodness.

Jesus told a story about a man who decided to throw an extravagant party for all of his closest friends. He wanted them to enjoy the best he had to offer. He sent the invitations and made all the preparations. He imported the finest foods and hired the best private chefs. He laid out a lavish table complete with china and fresh flowers. When it was time for the party to start, he sent private messengers to gather the guests. One by one they sent their regrets. Some were too busy conducting business. One said he couldn't come because he had just gotten married.

This made the man angry, so he sent his messengers back out to invite broken people—beggars, the homeless, addicts, and the poor. All of these people were thrilled to accept, and many came. The man then sent his messengers out again, urging them to go further from his home and compel more to come. He wanted his house filled with any who wanted to come and share in his elaborate feast.

Jesus told this "Parable of the Great Banquet" (Luke 14:15–24) to illustrate how God is extending His invitation to all. God is inviting everyone—the businessperson, homemaker, newlywed, poor, crippled, blind, lame, and outcast—to His eternal party.

Jesus personally invited many to follow Him. These followers, in turn, extended the invitation to others:

- Andrew invited Peter to meet Jesus (John 1:40–42).
- Philip invited Nathaniel to meet Jesus (John 1:43–46).
- The Samaritan woman invited her whole town to meet Jesus (John 4:28–30).
- Matthew (Levi) gave a feast to introduce Jesus to all his friends (Luke 5:27–29).
- Cornelius invited his family and friends to hear the gospel (Acts 10:24–33).

God is making His appeal through us (2 Cor. 5:20). Remember, we are only responsible for the invitation, we aren't responsible for the response. Just as many in Jesus' story refused the invitation to the great banquet, many will refuse our invitations. This shouldn't keep us from inviting. We can learn how to turn the rejections into opportunities for future gospel conversations.

Three Gospel Hinges

The invitation is the third of three primary gospel conversation hinges.

1. *Transition Question*—We gave an example, and you have developed and practiced your own (chapter 4).
2. *Gospeling Tool*—Evangelists around the world have found our 3 Circles to be reproducible and reproducing. The key is training with a lot of repetition.
3. *Invitation*—We end our 3 Circles conversation by asking the person with whom we are sharing where he or she sees him- or herself within the 3 Circles. Many will identify with the place of brokenness, but regardless of where they see themselves, we issue an invitation. We ask, "Is there anything that would keep you from repenting and believing the gospel right now?"

Training

It's human nature to be hesitant anytime we aren't sure what might happen next. Very few of us would even contemplate putting on a wet suit, getting a few air tanks, and making a go at deep-sea diving. Even fewer would rent a plane and parachute to give skydiving a whirl. If we want to attempt activities that have life-or-death consequences, we're probably going to sign up for lessons. We're going to practice on the shore or on the ground. We're going to try it first with someone who is a skilled diver or parachutist. Then, after a good bit of training and practice, we'll go for it.

We live in a diverse and complex society, which is why many of us are hesitant to engage in gospel conversations. We wonder what we'll say if the person is an atheist or a Shiite Muslim, or grew up as a Mormon. What if he or she is a physicist and asks us our views on the theory of quantum entanglement? We may be tempted to spend years training and preparing for every possible argument and objection.

The truth is there are really only three responses to the gospel. If we can train people how to deal with these three responses, then we can give them the confidence needed to engage in gospel conversations.

Three Responses

The three responses are red light, yellow light, and green light. Acts 17:32–34 (ESV) says, "Now when they heard of the resurrection of the dead, some mocked. But others said, 'We will hear you again about this.' So Paul went out from their midst. But some men joined him and believed."

- Red light—some mocked.
- Yellow light—some said, "We will hear you again."
- Green light—some joined and believed.

We can be prepared for each of these responses. We'll give you examples of how to handle each of them. But, again, we encourage you to personalize them. After you feel comfortable with your responses to each response, practice them! We often have people pair off and create scenarios with each other. They practice sharing the 3 Circles, the invitation, and how to handle each of the three responses. This may seem too scripted or even silly. You may be thinking that the Holy Spirit will just give you the words to say when you need them. Often, He will. But it's also the Holy Spirit's job to remind us of what we know. If our golf swing is worth practicing, then certainly our gospel sharing is as well!

Green Light: "Yes" Response

This is the response we're always hoping and praying to get. When someone says he or she is ready to repent and believe, we simply lead that person in a verbal expression of his or her inward heart change. There is no magical prayer that seals the deal on a person's eternal destiny. The Bible says if we believe in our hearts that God raised Jesus from the dead *and* confess with our mouths that He is Lord, we will be saved (Rom. 10:9). It says all who call on the name of the Lord will be saved (Rom. 10:13). We want to help people confess with their mouths and call on the Lord.

We can model for them a short prayer: "God, I know I'm a sinner and I'm broken. Please forgive me of my sins and make me whole. I believe Jesus died on the cross and rose from the dead. I'm asking Him to come into my life right now to help me recover and pursue God's design for my life." We always ask them to pray after us or with us.

Here are some reports of green light responses:

Last night after I shared the 3 Circles with two people, they accepted Jesus as their Lord and Savior. I am working with their schedules to see how to get them baptized.

Just had a friend accept Christ!!! I have been praying for this one over ten months now.

I shared the 3 Circles with someone at work, one of our clients who has never been a person of a faith, and we begin the discipleship on Monday! He's fired up.

My wife and I shared the 3 Circles with a young couple, and they accepted Jesus as their Savior and want to be discipled.

Led a lady to the Lord tonight using the 3 Circles. When I was talking about sin, she asked me if God forgives people who have sinned a lot. Shared the Simon story, and she started crying.

I drove out to see my cousin for dinner while she's on a business trip and took her through the 3 Circles. She gave her life to Christ!!! So exciting!!!

At lunch today I shared my testimony, the 3 Circles, and the story of the prodigal son. She said yes!

Yellow Light: "I need to think about it" Response

Many times the people with whom we share are enticed by the gospel, but they're hesitant to accept. They're open to what they've heard, but they're not ready to repent and believe. We take this at face value. However, we also realize that it may be a long time before these people are in another gospel conversation. We may want to challenge their thinking by asking them when they last had a conversation about Jesus or eternity. This helps them realize how the opportunities are few and far between. It may serve to draw them in and motivate them to take action.

We could also say something like this: "You mentioned you need to think about this some more, and I think that's a great idea. I get together with some friends once a week [every other week or once a month] to talk about life and God. We would love to have you join us." This invitation keeps the conversation going.

Ed Stetzer has found that 42–61 percent of non-Christians would be willing to study the Bible with a friend.[23] He also posited that 75–89 percent would listen

98

to someone share his or her faith.[24] People are more open than we might think. God is working on their hearts and drawing them to His Son, Jesus.

Here are some reports of yellow light responses:

I got to share the 3 Circles with Brian, the waiter at dinner, and prayed with him—he's keen to learn more about God.

Did not have a napkin during break, so I drew the 3 Circles on the concrete for my mechanic and went over it with him. A couple of people have stopped and looked at it since. Hopefully it doesn't rain.

I shared the 3 Circles with my neighbor, and while she believes in Jesus, she isn't ready to give control of her life over to Him. She did say she'd be open to studying the Bible with me.

> I just left my oncologist, so I figured I would give you guys the update. I'm showing advances that surpass our knowledge. I told her the other medicine I take is called a daily dose of Jesus. She asked what I meant, so I shared the 3 Circles with her and exchanged cell phone numbers with her. If you know about doctors, they never give out their personal cell phone numbers. She was very open and receptive. Let's pray!!

> We purchased a minivan today. Got to share the gospel using 3 Circles with the owner (an atheist Russian Jewish orphan who grew up in communism) while drawing up paper work. He stopped me and invited his whole staff and another customer to come and listen. He didn't believe but wants to continue the conversation.

Red Light: "No" Response

That's right—some people will respond negatively to the message that God loves them and has made a way out of their brokenness. We believe we should respond graciously to a "no." There should be no arguing, debating, or celestial moves in Christian apologetics as if we're involved in a cosmic chess match—none of that. We train people to say something like this: "Thank you for listening to me. If you ever find yourself in a place of brokenness, please remember our conversation and that God has made a way out through His Son, Jesus." This is a great red light response. Often people ask to keep the napkin or piece of paper with the 3 Circles on it, so who knows how God may use it?

Here are just a few red light responses:

> Started the tattoo work today. Shared the 3 Circles with the artist and invited him to church. I got a yellow light, but we have several more weeks together to work on him. I shared it with one of the other artists there and got a fat red light.

> I was able to share the gospel with my waitress today. She wasn't interested—red light.

I finally worked up the nerve to share the gospel with my dad who I've been praying for, but I didn't get the response I hoped for.

Shared the 3 Circles with my neighbor at the pool. He shut me down pretty good.

Invitations Are Powerful

Please don't neglect to issue the invitation or to train others to do the same. God, through His servant Joshua, urged people to "choose this day whom you will serve" (Josh. 24:15 ESV). Jesus repeatedly invited people, saying simply, "Follow Me" (Mark 1:17; 2:14; 8:34; 10:21, etc.). He then told the story of the great banquet so that His followers would know the inviting was up to them. Paul begged Herod to believe in Jesus (Acts 26:27–29) and then urged us to implore others to be reconciled to God through Jesus (2 Cor. 5:20).

It's great to share the gospel, but we must not forget that the gospel demands a response. If we're going to multiply disciples, we need people who are rapid to accept the invitation and rapid to go out and invite others.

CHAPTER SEVEN

Rapid Obedience

Think for a moment of all the serious hurdles, difficulties, and persecution the early church faced. Their founder was gone. They had no Bible or Christian literature. There were no seminaries to attend. They had no buildings, headquarters, or denominational support. The leaders they did have were uneducated, untested, and full of doubt. It had only been a few months since one of their most prominent leaders denied knowing Jesus and another committed suicide. Yet with all that was against the church, it did much more than simply survive—it exploded! How?

Peter, the serial denier, was filled with the Holy Spirit and preached the gospel, and "that day about 3,000 people were added to them" (Acts 2:41). The Jerusalem believers began to gather, and the first church was planted. From there, they continued to meet together, "and every day the Lord added to them those who were being saved" (Acts 2:47). These ordinary, new believers were being faithful to Jesus' mission. They went and started gospel conversations, made disciples, baptized them, and taught them to obey Jesus' commands.

Acts 4:4 records the results: "But many of those who heard the message believed, and the number of the men came to about 5,000." It is not long before multiplication breaks out. Acts 5:14 (ESV) says that "multitudes" believed, and Acts 6:7 (ESV) says "the number of the disciples multiplied greatly in Jerusalem." Please don't miss this—these are new believers telling others about the death, burial, and resurrection of Jesus. Their daily gospel conversations result in people daily repenting and believing the gospel. They are sowing much seed—telling everyone they encounter about Jesus' ability to forgive sin.

The movement seems contained to Jerusalem at first, and Saul—a prominent Jewish religious leader—is tenaciously doing his best to squash it. He oversees the stoning of Stephen (Acts 7), which puts the Jerusalem believers on the run. This incident is the catalyst that scatters the new believers who had started to gather. The persecution that was meant to stop the gospel caused it to spread like wildfire. They continue to talk, share, and turn everyday conversations into gospel conversations. They go and begin to tell the surrounding communities about Jesus, who died for their sins, was buried, and rose from the dead. Then, Jesus appears to Saul at the worst possible time—at least from Saul's perspective. He is on his way to Damascus to persecute more Christians. Saul the persecutor is transformed into Paul the missionary. The movement spreads. Ordinary people filled with the Holy Spirit telling the gospel message are turning the world upside down.

Charles Spurgeon once said, "Every Christian is either a missionary or an imposter."[25] Multiplying movements ignite when new believers are immediately trained, discipled, and released to win and disciple those who are far from God. Jesus commissioned His followers to teach people to *obey* His commands, not just know them. Over the years, the American church has successfully imparted a lot of biblical knowledge, but have we been as successful when it comes to reinforcing obedience?

Converted to Commissioned

In Acts and throughout the New Testament, disciples were people who repented and believed in Jesus and immediately joined His mission to tell others. They weren't perfect. They didn't have it all together. They made mistakes and were often a theologically mixed bag. But they were clear on two things: the gospel's transformative power and their role as ambassadors.

Recently a young man moved to West Palm Beach from Pennsylvania to receive treatment for his severe heroin addiction. One of our church members shared the gospel with him using the 3 Circles, and he immediately repented and believed in Jesus. This young man was then immediately challenged to look for opportunities to turn conversations about life and its many problems into conversations about the gospel. He went back to his half-way house and, twenty-four hours later, reported that he had shared the gospel seven times. It turns out he knew a lot of broken people.

Some may argue that this is a risky strategy—letting a new believer go out and share the gospel. It may be risky, but it's also biblical. God records for us a number of examples where those who heard and believed imme-diately went and had gospel conversations.

- There is Levi, the tax collector, who immediately left everything to follow Jesus. Then he held a banquet at his house and invited everyone he knew to come and meet Jesus (Luke 5:27–32).

- There is Zaccheus, another wealthy tax collec-tor, who immediately welcomed Jesus gladly, and he and his whole household were saved (Luke 19:1–10).

- There is the woman whom Jesus met by the well one day—the one who had five previous husbands and was currently living with a man who wasn't her husband. Once she realized Jesus was the Messiah, she went and told everyone in her town, and "many Samaritans from that town believed in Him because of what the woman said when she testified, 'He told me everything I ever did'" (John 4:39).

- There is the demon-possessed man whom Jesus encountered in Gerasenes. Jesus cast the demons out of him and set him back to his right mind. The man wanted to stay with Jesus, but Jesus told him to go and tell his friends how much God had done for him and how He had mercy on him. The man obeyed Jesus. He immediately "went out and began to proclaim in the Decapolis how much Jesus had done for him, and they were all amazed" (Mark 5:20).

- God sent Peter to the home of a God-fearing Gentile named Cornelius, who invited all his friends and relatives to his home to hear what Peter had to say. "While Peter was still speaking these words, the Holy Spirit came down on all who heard the message. . . . And he commanded them to be baptized in the name of Jesus Christ.

Then they asked him to stay for a few days" (Acts 10:44, 48).

- There is the Philippian jailer in Acts 16:31–34 who asked Paul and Silas what he must do to be saved: "So they said, 'Believe on the Lord Jesus, and you will be saved—you and your household.' Then they spoke the message of the Lord to him along with everyone in his house. He took them the same hour of the night and washed their wounds. Right away he and all his family were baptized. He brought them into his house, set a meal before them, and rejoiced because he had believed God with his entire household."

- Also in Acts 16 is the story of a businesswoman named Lydia who heard the gospel, repented, believed, and was baptized along with her whole household. Once Paul and Silas were released from jail, we're told that they went to Lydia's house to meet with the other believers (Acts 16:40).

When we tell new believers that they're part of God's redemptive plan, they're humbled and eager to be trained and equipped as ambassadors. They're willing to rapidly obey Jesus' command to "go . . . and make disciples" (Matt. 28:19).

Train and Send

We need to follow the biblical model of discipleship: observe, train, and release. For example, Apollos had clear ministry giftedness and began to speak boldly in the synagogue. Yet when Priscilla and Aquila heard him, they took him aside and explained to him the way of God more accurately. Then, when he wished to cross to Achaia, the other believers encouraged him and wrote to the disciples to welcome him. He then greatly helped those who through grace had believed as he powerfully refuted the Jews in public, showing by the Scriptures that Jesus was the Messiah (Acts 18:26–28). There is no "new and improved" version of this basic discipleship pattern. There are no 2.0 upgrades. The goal is to mimic Jesus' method of discipleship, which is timeless and eternal.

We train people to turn everyday conversations in gospel conversations just as we have laid out here. We practice with them. We ask them to begin by praying for those they know who are far from God. We ask them to look for opportunities to transition to the gospel. We ask them to share the 3 Circles and offer an invitation to repent and believe. We train them to deal with the various responses. We hold them accountable, asking them to send us a text or e-mail or to give us a quick call when they have been obedient in doing what Jesus commanded them to do. We celebrate their stories and use them to encourage others. Salvation stories inspire us, allow us to rejoice with the angels in heaven, and help us remember how God is reconciling the world to Himself.

We are beginning to see multiplication in our South Florida mission context. Multiplication happens when we train ordinary, everyday missionaries to generously sow gospel seeds in the places they live, work, and play. We can't multiply if we constrain the gospel to a message that is shared exclusively on Sunday mornings or at big rallies. Churches that want to gauge multiplication can consider the following questions:

- How are we expanding vision for our people?
- How are we encouraging focused prayer?
- Are our gospeling tools simple and reproducible?
- Is there an abundance of gospel seed sowing?
- How are we training our people frequently and intentionally?
- Are new believers rapid to obey and go make disciples?
- Are we seeing generational growth?
- How are we holding each other accountable in loving ways?
- How are we celebrating stories?
- How are we multiplying churches?

Where Do We Start?

Every day, we encounter some people who are disciples of Jesus and others who are far from God. This means we have two opportunities every day:

1. Train disciples of Jesus to make disciples. It's as easy as TGI:

> Transition—Train believers to transition everyday conversations to gospel conversations. Train them and let them practice.
> Gospel—Train believers to use the 3 Circles as a conversation guide to lead people to the gospel.
> Invitation—Train believers to ask a direct invitation question. When we share good news, we want to invite a response.

2. Tell people far from God the good news. This means we have to be ready. We need to practice and get our reps in today so that we're in shape and ready to go when the opportunity arises.

In fact, let's make a list right now. Fill in the chart below with names of people you know who are far from God:

PEOPLE	PLACES	PASSIONS

Now pray for these people. We can add them to our daily prayer calendars. We can set an alarm on our phones to remind us to pray for them every day. We can set a time to meet with them and tell them something that has changed our lives.

There is no time like the present. Let's train ourselves and train others to turn everyday conversations into gospel conversations.

Appendix

Generational Discipleship Map:

Resources

3 Circle Training Kit
namb.net

3 Circles App
lifeonmissionbook.com/conversation-guide

Follow on Twitter
@JimmyScroggins
@SteveWright_

Share Your Stories
#3Circles

About The Authors

Jimmy Scroggins serves as the lead pastor of Family Church in West Palm Beach, Florida. Jimmy is married to Kristin, and they are blessed with eight children—James, Daniel, Jeremiah, Isaac, Stephen, Anna Kate, Mary Claire, and Caleb. Jimmy earned his PhD from The Southern Baptist Theological Seminary in Louisville, Kentucky. He is dedicated to building families in South Florida through a network of neighborhood churches. His vision is to see each Family Church campus on mission to help people in their community discover and pursue God's design. The Family Church Network has a vision to plant one hundred churches in South Florida.

Steve Wright serves as pastor of discipleship and church planting at Family Church in West Palm Beach, Florida. Steve is married to Tina, and they are blessed with three children—Sara, William, and Tyler. Steve earned his PhD from The Southern Baptist Theological Seminary in Louisville, Kentucky. He is also the author of *ApParent Privilege* (Family Discipleship) and *reThink— Decide for Yourself: Is Student Ministry Working?* Steve is passionate about multiplying disciples and desires that every resident in South Florida have repeated gospel conversations.

Notes

1. United States Census Bureau, "America's Families and Living Arrangements: 2014: Children (C Table Series)," accessed May 11, 2015, http://www.census.gov/hhes/families/data/cps2014C.html.

2. Tamara Halle, "Charting Parenthood: A Statistical Portrait of Fathers and Mothers in America," last modified June 9, 2006, http://fatherhood.hhs.gov/charting02/executive.htm.

3. Harris Poll, "The 2014 Consumer Financial Literacy Survey," accessed June 13, 2015, https://www.nfcc.org/wp-content/uploads/2013/06/NFCC_2014-FinancialLiteracySurvey_FINAL.pdf.

4. National Institute on Drug Abuse, "Nationwide Trends," accessed June 13, 2015, http://www.drugabuse.gov/publications/drugfacts/nationwide-trends.

5. Pew Research Center, "America's Changing Religious Landscape," May 12, 2015, http://www.pewforum.org/religious-landscape-study/age-distribution/18-29.

6. Frank Newport, "In U.S., Four in 10 Report Attending Church in Last Week," *Gallup*, December 24, 2013, http://www.gallup.com/poll/166613/four-report-attending-church-last-week.aspx.

7. Pew Research Center, "America's Changing Religious Landscape," May 12, 2015, http://www.pewforum.org/2015/05/12/americas-changing-religious-landscape.

8. North American Mission Board, "Regional Focus: South," accessed April 25, 2015, http://www.namb.net/south.

9. Barna Group, "What Are the Least Churched Cities in the U.S.?" April 24, 2015, http://cities.barna.org/barna-cities-the-top-churchless-metro-areas.

10. CBS News, "A Dying Breed: The American Shopping Mall," March 23, 2014, http://www.cbsnews.com/news/a-dying-breed-the-american-shopping-mall.

11. Jonathan Edwards, *Thoughts on the Revival of Religion in New England in 1740* (New York, NY: American Tract Society, 1735), 427.

12. Ibid., 46.

13. Ibid., 65.

14. Ibid., 68.

15. Ibid., 99.

16. Ibid., 65.

17. Bruce W. Frier, "Demography," in Alan K. Bowman, Peter Garnsey, and Dominic Rathbone, eds., *The Cambridge Ancient History XI: The High Empire, A.D. 70–192* (Cambridge: Cambridge University Press, 2000), 812.

18. Josh McDowell, *Evidence That Demands a Verdict* (San Bernadino, CA: Here's Life Publishers, Inc., 1986), 198–99.

19. Grace Stott, *Twenty-Six Years of Missionary Work in China* (New York, NY: American Tract Society, 1897), 3.

20. "New Survey Reveals Average Brit Has 27 Conversations Every Day," *Newswire Today*, August 26, 2010, http://www.news-wiretoday.com/news/76151/New-Survey-Reveals-Average-Brit-Has-27-Conversations-Every-Day.

Notes

21. Nikhil Swaminathan, "Gender Jabber: Do Women Talk More than Men?" *Scientific American*, July 6, 2007, http://www.scientificamerican.com/article/women-talk-more-than-men.

22. The North American Mission Board released this tool as the "3 Circles: Life Conversation Guide" in 2014. Their printed guide, app, and training videos are available at lifeonmissionbook.com.

23. Ed Stetzer, *Lost and Found* (Nashville, TN: B&H Publishing Group and Lifeway Research, 2009), Table 4.

24. Ibid.

25. Charles Spurgeon, ed., *The Sword and the Trowel* (London, UK: Passmore & Alabaster, 1873), 127.